DOING IT FOR THE KIDS

THE SUSTAINABLE
TOY STORY

ISBN: 978-0-9557129-2-0
Copyright 2009 Redesigndesign Limited
Published by Redesigndesign Limited t/a [re]design

[re]design
1 Summit Way, Crystal Palace, London SE19 2PU, England, UK

www.redesigndesign.org

for Milly, Max and little makers everywhere

INTRODUCTION

Play is in every child's nature – its how we learn about the world. If not given toys children will appropriate whatever they can find to become a toy, a plaything. We don't need to teach kids how to play, but we can help facilitate this instinct by giving them good, green toys.

Good toys help children to develop physical, mental and social skills. They allow children to play freely and learn about the world. They spark imaginations and mould values. They are kind to the environment and foster a sense of fun, enjoyment and care for others. They help make us better people.

As designers, sustainability educators, play enthusiasts and parents we have been decidedly unimpressed by the toy offer currently put forward by major UK retailers. The market is dominated by over-packaged, over-hyped, over-merchandised, stifling designs. Convinced there must be some better – more sustainable, more flexible, more playable, more lovable – alternatives out there, we went searching.

We looked around the world for play design demonstrating relevance, good design, positive play values, green materials, eco packaging, and lifecycle consideration. The dearth of examples from the big toy names is both sad and frustrating; and the widespread industry obsession with chasing the latest IP license completely lacking in imagination. But our toy trawl did uncover lots of innovative little elves working away, whom together could have a big impact.

Collectively, the Doing It For The Kids products demonstrate an alternative pathway for play design. The approaches from the designers are diverse, and the range of projects included together build a rich picture of the possibilities of positive, greener play.

The toys we give our children say a lot about our society. We hope that Doing It For The Kids will inspire you – child, designer, educator, carer, parent or grandparent – to be more knowledgeable, critical, confident and creative in your play choices.

Play away!

Sarah and Jason
[re]design

WHO'S DOING IT FOR THE KIDS...

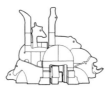

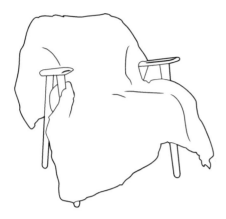

Dimensions (cm): H190 W150 D2
Target Age: 4+
Play Type: Copying
[re]strategies: [re]cycle, [re]create
Materials: Second-hand dolls clothes, found parachute,
second-hand T-shirts, organic cotton wadding,
cotton thread

8 **ACTION MAN & BARBIE QUILT**
KATHERINE MAY

As designers we need to encourage people to engage and form relationships with our products.

Having more knowledge about products can leave us feeling empowered and move us away from throwaway habits.

Ever wondered what happened to your childhood Barbie's glam frocks? Or those Action Man combats? They could well be enjoying a new lease of life as an Action Man or Barbie Quilt.

Created by textile designer Katherine May, each unique quilt, as well as being a work of art, is a fantastical visual and tactile toy. Use it to comfort, hide under, encourage single or group play; or as camouflage for a den or a shiny roof for a palace. They're also great for dreaming under at night!

Katherine's philosophy is to bring the 'emotionally durable object into the everyday' and pass on her passion of traditional textile skills. And with each quilt being passed on through generation to generation - patched up and made good by new hands - the quilts will enjoy a long life and do their bit to preserve craft skills.

Where are the shorts in the Action Man Quilt?

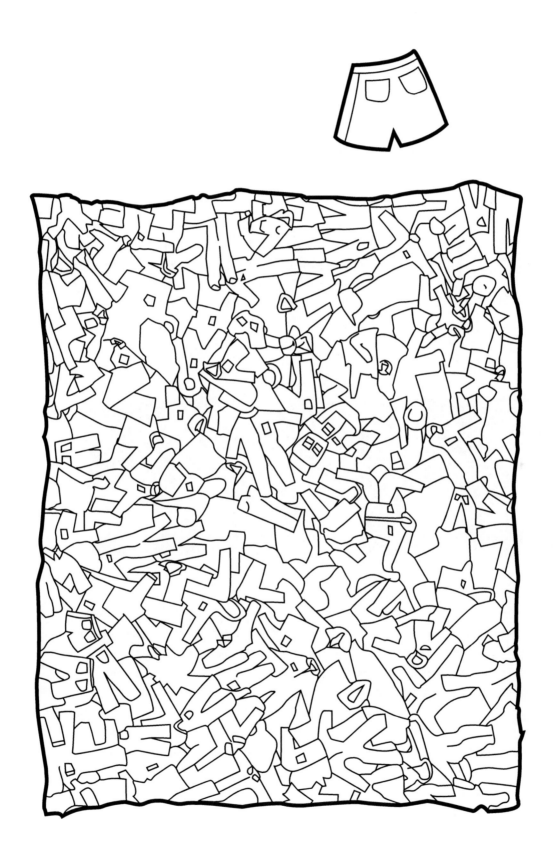

Dimensions (cm): H27 W14 D18
Target Age: 3-5
Play Type: Copying, Head Spin
[re]strategies: [re]cycle, [re]duce, [re]spond
Materials: Sprigwood - recycled plastics, wood flour

I try to create toys that have just enough in them to get the kid's imagination started, then get out of their way and let them play.

10 ADVENTURE SERIES
SPRIG TOYS

Active kids, happy parents, healthy planet.
What a wonderful world.

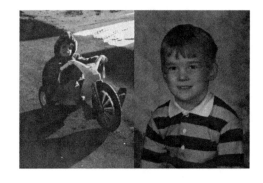

Who needs batteries when you've got the ultimate energy resource – children?
The Adventure Series is a inspiring new play concept from the Sprig Toys team – Chris, Craig, David and Justin. The Adventure Series Discover Rig is an ingenious thing indeed – it harnesses the energy of a child as it trundles on a crazy safari caper through deepest Africa. When an adventurer rolls the vehicle forward, it triggers the dynamo that fuels the lights and sounds. Powering the Discover Rig

is, quite literally, child's play! It's not just the power that's environmentally friendly, the primary material in all the Adventure Series models is Sprigwood - a biocomposite made from recycled plastics and wood, and all packaging is made from vegetable printed recycled material. There are five adventure characters, led by Cap Faraday. And with songs, dialogue, motor noise and a range of hilarious animal sounds round every corner, it promises to be a thrilling kid-powered ride.

What have the Adventure Team discovered?

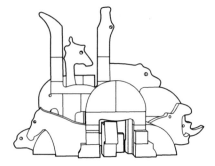

Dimensions (cm): H9 W15 D2
Target Age: 2-8
Play Type: Copying, Self-Expression
[re]strategies: [re]source, [re]spond
Materials: Locally forested beech, water-based dyes,
water-based paints

12 **ANIMAL CITY**
CHARLIE DAVIDSON

Design isn't just about making pretty objects. Design is a process that draws on every aspect of our lives to make more intelligent and considered products. Design can introduce new solutions to consumption and what we really need in life.

Drawing cats and playing with wooden blocks with two year-old daughter Astrid inspired Sweden-based designer Charlie Davidson to create the Animal City building blocks. Stackable wooden blocks based around a bear, a horse, a rhino, a crocodile and other animal shapes encourage children to learn about different animals and think up their own invented creatures by jumbling up the shapes. Developed using a CAD (computer-aided design) drafting package, the Animal City pieces are designed to be made from locally forested beech wood cut with a CNC (computer numerical controlled) router. Each piece has minimum surface finishing; they are waxed or stained using water based products.

So what makes a toy truly sustainable? For Charlie, who grew up loving Lego and cardboard boxes, it's a quality toy that can be passed on, offering great playability - that's the key.

Can you make an animal?

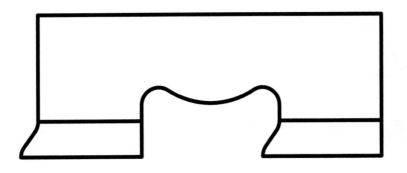

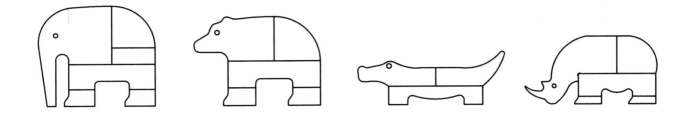

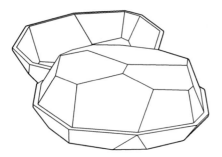

Dimensions (cm): H5 W6 D9
Target Age: 3+
Play Type: Head Spin, Self-Expression
[re]strategies: [re]duce, [re]source, [re]spond
Materials: Plastarch material (PSM), chalk

14 **APOD**
IAN MAHAFFY INDUSTRIAL DESIGN

The message translated to the child through the unpacking and disposal of excess toy packaging is a disturbing one and is not the message we want to teach our children in regards to sustainability.

Designers Ian Mahaffy and Louise Hedegaard Madsen wanted to show that packaging can be useful, have an afterlife, and even become part of the play itself.

A crystal-shaped shell holding a large chalk for creative and inspiring physical play outdoors, APOD protects its chalk when being transported, and becomes a stone or throwing piece during play.

The APOD's faceted shape resembles the form a lump of chalk becomes as it is used, so the APOD player will feel that they are adding to its form rather than destroying it in use.

APOD casing is designed to be injection-moulded from Plastarch material (PSM). Play continues online, where a street chalk community can share street game ideas, instructions and upload street chalk art.

Can you complete the hopscotch court and play with your fingers?

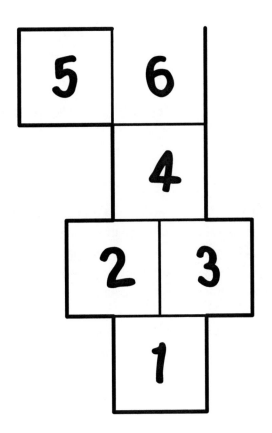

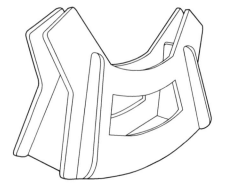

Dimensions (cm): H71 W45 D37
Target Age: 3-7
Play Type: Head Spin, Self-Expression
[re]strategies: [re]cycle, [re]create, [re]spond
Materials: Corrugated cardboard

16 **BILLY ROCKER**
MR KALISKI

Since becoming a father, my attention has been on making sustainable products for my children.

Teaching sustainability through a toy will have great benefits for future generations.

The Billy Rocker is no mere rocking horse – after all, why limit your child's play to just one animal?

Billy Rocker takes its inspiration from German designer Walter Papst, who designed 'Rocking Sculpture' in the 1950s, and made a deliberate point of not restricting imagination by means of a name. Designer Adam Kay's playful interactive rocker is aimed at three to seven year-olds and is made from four-ply die cut cardboard which is glued to make a solid form and then slotted together. The frame is left deliberately 'head and tail free' allowing kids to customise and create their own real or fantasy creatures.

A dragon with a dog's tail? A bunny with a crocodile's tail? Or how about the head of a rockabilly with the tail of a billy goat? That's up to the mind of its little owner!

What creature would you like to rock on?

Dimensions (cm): H25 W25 D25
Target Age: 3-7
Play Type: Discovery, Head to Head
[re]strategies: [re]source, [re]spond
Materials: Organic cotton, herbal dye,
rubberised coconut fibres

18 **BIRDIE NUM NUM**
NIELS PETER FLINT

The Birdie Num Nums are 'catalystic toys', they will hopefully get kids and parents to play and talk and think about our relationship to nature.

Everything as a starting point needs to be redeveloped and redesigned for tomorrow's sustainable world.

Have you ever seen a pig-bird, peacock-fish, elephant-bird, or snake-rooster? They might not exist yet, but GM technology may well make it possible one day. Until then, the Birdie Num Num toys can give you an early insight into how these creatures could look. The Birdie Num Nums are genetically modified creatures; a fusion of two animals. Fun, yet with a serious message... Big enough for small kids to sit on, Birdie Num Nums encourage both children and parents to

engage in play and communicate to consider serious issues such as genetic modification in general and the ethics of meat production in particular. The toys can encourage creative sustainability as kids develop new Birdie creations.

The products, made from organic cotton and rubberised coconut fibres, are made on a small production facility in Gujarat, India. At end of life they can happily be composted.

Can you invent a Birdie Num Num using features from two animals?

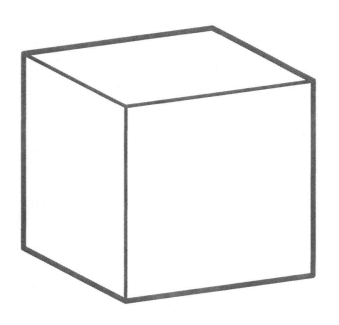

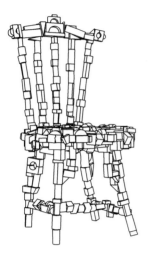

Dimensions (cm): H95 W45 D45
Target Age: Any age
Play Type: Self-Expression
[re]strategies: [re]mind, [re]use
Materials: Wood, glue

20 **BRICK CHAIR**
PEPE HEYKOOP

Looking at a material in a different way, just imagine building the things you like.

The mass of choice in products that do not have any quality annoys me a lot.

Pepe Heykoop's surreal Brick Chair looks like it could have magicked its way from the fairytale sweetie cottage in Hansel and Gretel, apearing good enough to eat.

But it's so much more than that – because it's good enough to seat as well…

The Brick Chair was inspired by a drawing made by illustrator James Gulliver Hancock. But the leap from drawing to toy bricks is immense – it's hand-made from more than 1,000 second-hand toy bricks and takes 'lots and lots of hours' to complete.

Pepe takes pleasure in using materials already in existence that have a story behind them. And the wooden bricks can be recycled and go on to have a new life.

Time for a sit down.

Can you find the brick in the Brick Chair?

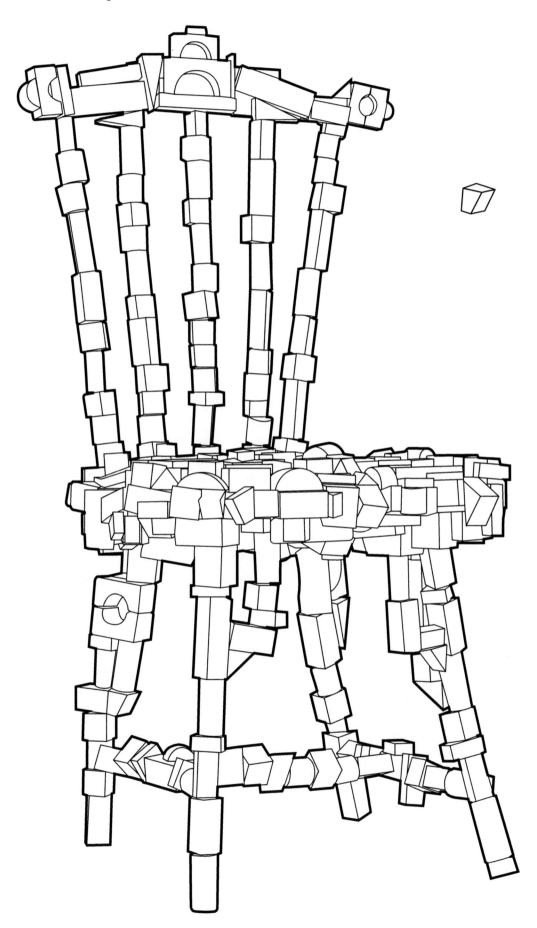

Dimensions (cm): Variable
Target Age: 3-99
Play Type: Copying, Self-Expression
[re]strategies: [re]source, [re]spond
Materials: European FSC & PEFC registered Pine, acrylic
paint (non-toxic, manufactured in the UK)

22 BUILDING BLOCKS
CHRISTOPHER JARRATT

What got me into sustainability was watching my grandad fix things, that to me, as a six year-old, looked totally broken.

I recently restored a beautiful wartime bicycle which is now back on the road with some new stories to tell, as well as many old ones.

A contemporary take on traditional wooden block sets, Christopher Jarratt's fun and funky Building Blocks promote play and stimulate the minds of little and big kids from three to 99. Multicoloured indoor cities, pastel parks, orange and green suburbs and pink mini sky-scrapers can be created and kids can even learn the art of good town planning by knocking up hand-drawn paper road networks. Christopher designs, makes and hand-screen prints Building Blocks from his Cornish studio using sustainably sourced registered pine and non-toxic acrylic inks. Hand-screen printing allows the blocks to pick up their own individual features, making each set entirely unique from any other.

Next in the Building Block pipeline is Christopher's plan to develop more pieces – people, animals, bikes, cars... the start of a small wooden world!

Can you finish designing the Eco City?

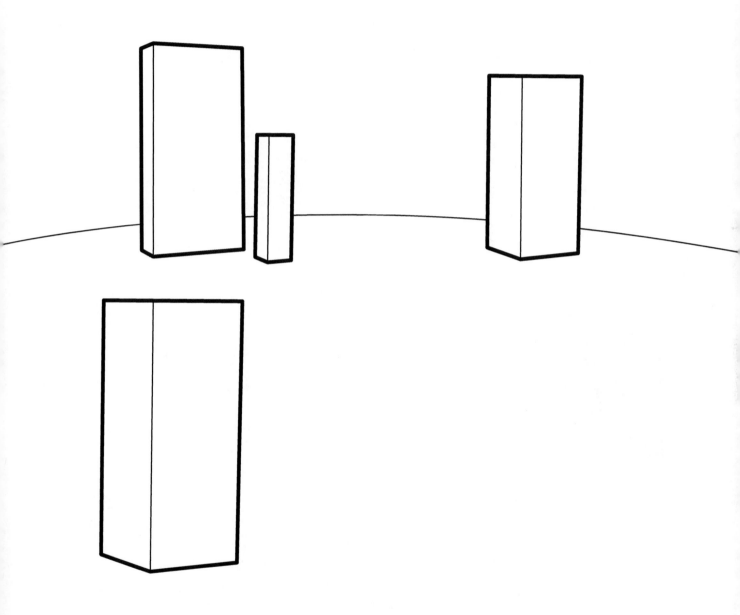

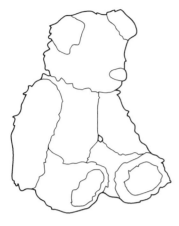

Dimensions (cm): H20 W22 D24
Target Age: Adults
Play Type: Chance, Copying
[re]strategies: [re]create, [re]mind
Materials: Glazed stoneware

24 **CERAMIC BEAR**
BODIL SÖDERLUND

Being a farmergirl, I am acutely aware of lifecycles – we are born, we live and we die. So does everything around us but only us humans have the imagination and skills to make things better or worse.

Make sure the things around you matter.

Even the best-loved teddy eventually falls apart – or gets shoved into the bottom of a box in the back of an attic – but here's a way you can breathe new life into him. Swedish designer Bodil Söderlund offers an individual service that can turn your dear battered old bear into a beautiful ceramic teddy. However, the transformation process is far from cool – the cuddly keepsake is restuffed with natural fibers and burnt at temperatures reaching 1,200 degrees. In sacrificing your old friend to the heat of the kiln you will be rewarded with a precious (if less cuddly) object that evokes memories of your childhood. By turning your redundant teddy bear into a beautiful sculpture full of history and emotional value, you give your old friend a new life, which bridges your childhood with your adult days. Minimal tooling and new materials are needed to make these unique, glazed ceramic bears, as the teddies themselves create the forms. Come on... let your teddy grow up!

Can you draw what is coming out of the Kiln?

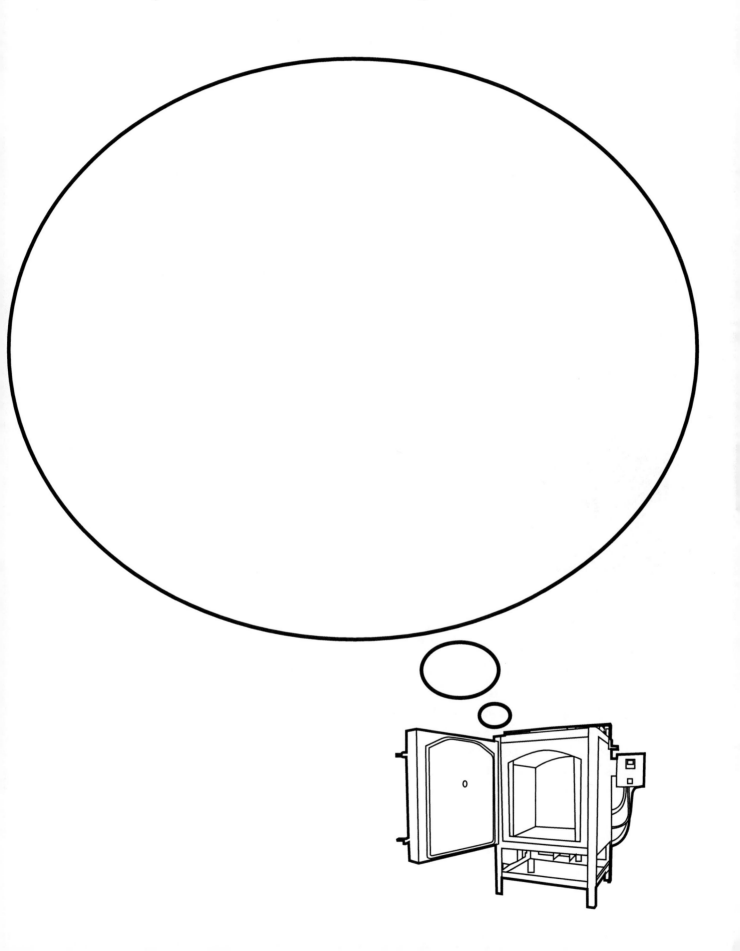

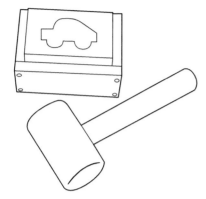

Dimensions (cm): H6 W16 D15
Target Age: 4-10
Play Type: Copying, Self-Expression
[re]strategies: [re]create, [re]cycle, [re]spond
Materials: Sycamore wood

26 **CITY MOULD**
HANNAH SCROGGS

Cardboard boxes were my favourite childhood toy, as they were always and will always be much more fun than real toys!

I create work which considers the portrayal of the adult world to children through toys.

City Mould lets kids make their own cities out of waste paper, encouraging creative and imaginative play and reinforcing a positive sustainable message from an early age. City Mould is a modular mould system enabling children to make solid paper cityscape shapes from old newspapers and water. No adhesive or additives are required. Children are encouraged to get hands-on, be resourceful and imaginative by creating their own play objects from waste material, decorating them in any way they choose… and assuming the role of town planner in deciding the ratio and location of trees, houses, caravans and tower blocks.

Designer Hannah Scroggs has made a product using commonplace materials and modern-day urban environments for play. Key to her product creation was enabling children to 'home manufacture' and encouraging them to think and debate.

Can you paint the town red, yellow, green, blue?

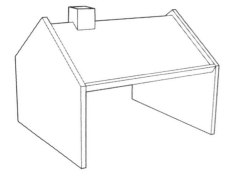

Dimensions (cm): H75 W100 D90
Target Age: 2-10
Play Type: Copying, Self-Expression
[re]strategies: [re]duce, [re]mind, [re]spond
Materials: Melamine laminated FSC plywood

28 **DESKHOUSE**
NINETONINE

Sustainability is an underlying issue for any sensitive and sensible person nowadays, be they designer, architect or other. But you begin to feel it even more keenly once you have children: their future might not be so bright unless we learn to look after it.

The Deskhouse embodies the universal drawing almost every child creates in nursery of the square house with its chimney and winding garden path – so children immediately relate to the symbolic shape of the design. The idea of the Deskhouse is to promote fun and sharing while playing, drawing, and studying. Encompassing both playtable and playhouse children enjoy using it to draw or read, as well as playing underneath it. Made from melamine laminated FSC plywood, it is available in two sizes for two or four children. Designer Alberto Marcos believes children can appreciate good, contemporary design and deserve to be surrounded by it from an early age. The design could potentially evolve with the addition of doors and windows, but given the omnipresence of garish plastic electronic toys with lights and noises that bombard children nowadays, Alberto imagines he'll leave Deskhouse as it is. Less is most definitely more in this case.

What will you do at the desk house?

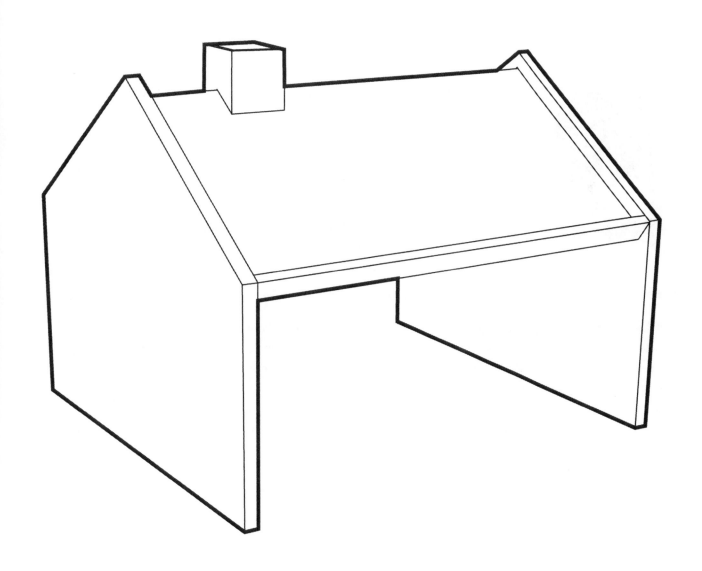

Dimensions (cm): H5 W5 D4
Target Age: 5-88
Play Type: Copying, Self-Expression
[re]strategies: [re]create, [re]spond , [re]use
Materials: Paper

30 **DIFTK PAPER TOY**
DOLLY OBLONG

It stimulates logical insight in building a 3D object out of a sheet of paper.

It's not every day free toys come your way but there are a whole bunch available by Dutch designer Dolly Oblong. Available online to download, children can print and build the paper toys themselves. Specially created for Doing It For The Kids, the DIFTK Paper Toy includes a sheet of ready-made parts but kids can also customise and add their own elements. The paper toy template can be printed on leftover scraps of paper – from magazines to wrapping paper, whatever

appeals. Kids can print out as many templates as they want for minimal printing costs. They are then cut, slotted and glued together.

Part of Dolly's Paper toy family, the DIFTK Paper Toy is easy to make and simple to customise to create a your own funky paper toy characters.

Can you design your own DIFTK Paper Toy?

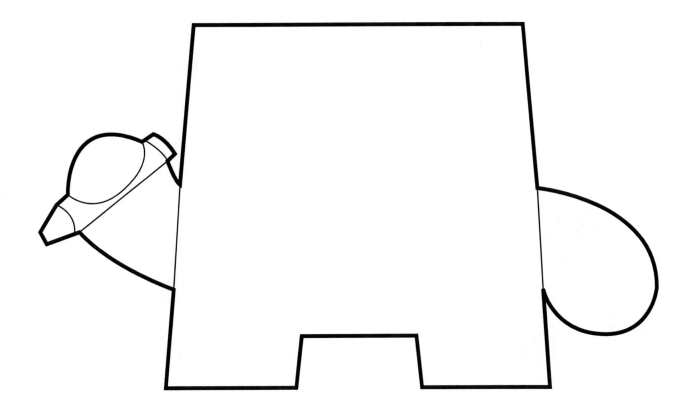

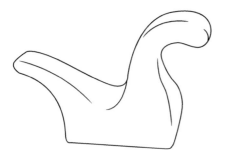

Dimensions (cm): H66 W35 D110 (Dino)
Target Age: 0-6
Play Type: Copying, Discovery, Headspin
[re]strategies: [re]spond
Materials: Fireproof sofficel® covered by washable, self-extinguishing and water-repellent ecosoftx® removable covers

DINO & 3D FORMS
ZPZ FOR PLAY+

In designing for children very often people seek to predict and control usage. PLAY+ tried to do this as little as possible. We believe that offering children the greatest number of opportunities possible for interpreting a place contributes to their development.

PLAY+ is a research project that creates soft furnishings for young children. Their lightweight multi-coloured 3D Forms let kids transform environments by constructing bright spaces, seating and partitions for role-play; whilst Dino is an animal form to ride, a seat, and a cushion to support safe dynamic play. The laboratory process involved the collaboration of 28 international designers – including the creators of Dino and 3D Forms, ZPZ Partners: Mattia, Michele, and Claudia –

working with the 'Children, spaces, relations' team of Reggio Children and Domus Academy in Italy. The PLAY+ collection of products includes soft 3D landscapes, animal shapes, transformable seating, play structures, mats, modular forms, burrows and shelters, all made from proprietary materials – sofficel®, a fireproof foam, and ecosoftx®, a synthetic PVC-free fabric covering that is soft to the touch, water-repellent, easy to clean, mould-resistant, odourless, and ecological.

Can you help Dino through the 3D Forms to reach his food?

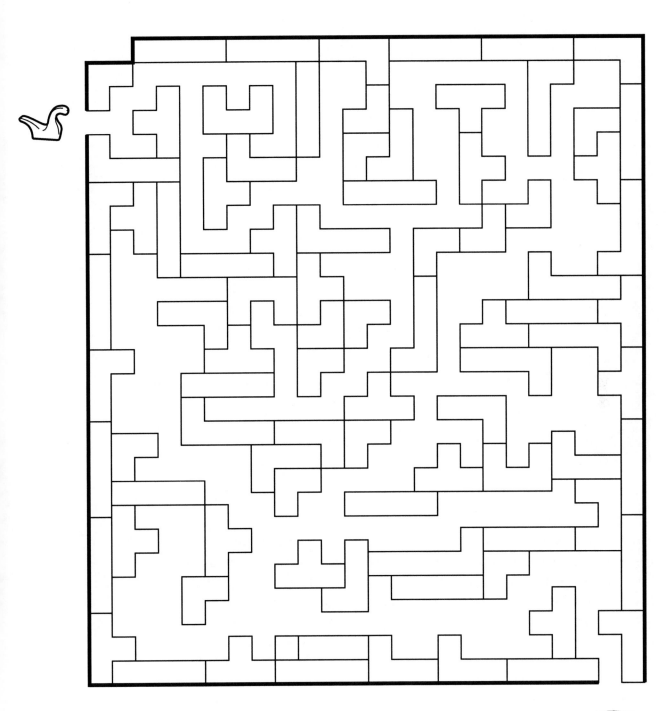

Dimensions (cm): H20 W10 D5
Target Age: 8-80
Play Type: Self-Expression
[re]strategies: [re]claim, [re]create, [re]mind
Materials: Vintage fabric, leftovers from garment factories

34　**DIWHY**
CHOCOLATE RAIN

Design is about d.i.y: determination, inspiration, y-not?

Obsessed with shiny objects and commercial success, young kids' thinking can be one-dimensional. Throughout the d.i.y. journey, they begin to reassess everything they took for granted.

A huge fan of upcycling vintage fabric, Hong Kong-based designer Prudence Mak doesn't get why anyone would want to throw out their old clothes. To her, throwing away clothes is like throwing away your memory – old garments are precious and a massive part of your personal history. Through their kits, Chocolate Rain hope to influence future generations to apply imagination to cast-off materials and to rethink society's over-consuming habits.

The diwhy kits themselves are hand-made, finished with a sewing machine and come in a variety of designs, from the Fatina character doll, a brooch, earrings, a pin cushion, keyring, make-up bag or tote bag. The kits contain vintage fabric and leftovers from garment factories – all you need to complete the diwhy kits are a needle, cotton and some of your own outgrown clothing. Kids aged eight upwards can discover how their old clothes can be turned into a wonderful toy or gift.

Can you design the clothes for Fatina?

Dimensions (cm): H22 W22 D22
Target Age: Any age
Play Type: Head Spin, Head to Head
[re]strategies: [re]duce, [re]spond, [re]use
Materials: Recycled cardboard

In life, and even in our surroundings, there are objects with traces of lapsed memories. Let us endow new life into these objects.

36 **DREAMBALL**
UNPLUG DESIGN

Pull out the plug from the system and plug in the community.

For many children living in third-world countries, buying toys would be an unthinkable luxury. But what if a toy could be made out of famine relief packaging? Seoul-based designers Hwang Kyung Chan, Jin Song Kyou, Lee Hak Su, Han Min Hyun and Jun Jin have found a smart way of redesigning relief packaging from the UN and Red Cross into Dreamball, a football of a different kind.

Cardboard packaging is perforated, to make it easy to tear. Pieces can be woven into different Dreamball sizes depending on the size of the boxes. It's a simple, effective idea that could help relief agencies deliver the positive power of play alongside food and medication. Everyone needs to play, and the Dreamball project offers hope and joy where it's most needed.

Does the Dreamball go in the goal?
You decide. Draw the goalkeeper.

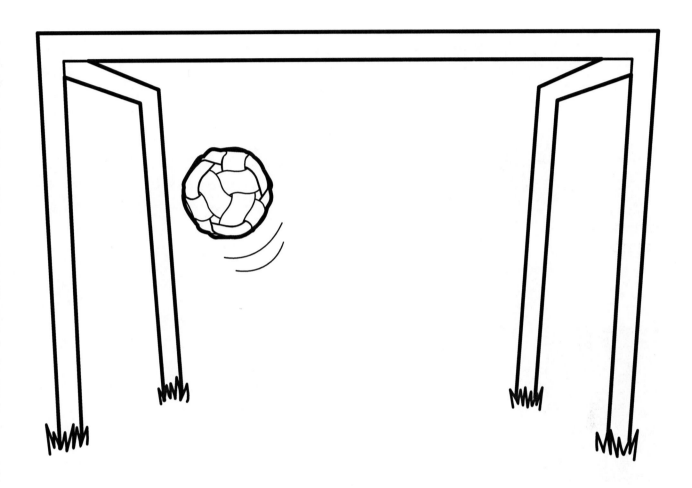

Dimensions (cm): H6 W7 D7
Target Age: 7-70
Play Type: Discovery
[re]strategies: [re]duce, [re]spond, [re]use
Materials: Silicone

38 **FAT BIRD**
REESTORE

I am inspired by watching people carry out everyday tasks in a haphazard manner. Problem-solving makes me happy.

Materials, interaction, education and end-of-life consideration are all highly important factors in toy design.

Birds love fat cakes… Encourage more feathered friends into your garden or local park, and get kids into wildlife with yummy Fat Bird DIY cakes.

Instead of pouring leftover cooking fat down the sink and blocking sewers, the Fat Bird DIY cake kits teach kids to care for wildlife and promote re-use. It's a great way for parents to interact with kids as well. Designer Max McMurdo hit on the idea while cooking and

getting frustrated with the lack of an eco-friendly way of disposing of excess fat.

The kit, made from 100% recyclable silicone, consists of a single funky cake mould with bird feet and is available in child-friendly colours. Just pour in your old fat, sprinkle in some seeds and leave to set. The cakes then easily pop out of the mould ready for hungry birds. Make sure those greedy robins share!

Who is eating the Fat Bird cake?

Dimensions (cm): H50 W30 D1
Target Age: 7-77
Play Type: Copying, Self-Expression
[re]strategies: [re]mind, [re]spond
Materials: Wool, cotton thread, plastic elements (optional)

40   **FORGET ME KNOT THE MONSTER SCARF**
AMELIE LABARTHE

Children are rebels. They won't necessarily have fun with what and where you expect them to, the whole challenge is to try and meet them in a place where their freedom of imagination is respected.

Forget Me Knot is a super-long, super-soft scarf full of monsters that come to life when you knot it. The scarf promotes a playful and creative attitude towards an object. It encourages you to let things go, as each time you unknot the scarf you lose the character you designed, but you will always be able to come up with a new one. It fosters creativity and develops a user's confidence in their actions. The scarf also engenders emotional durability. It is comforting, adaptable and characterful – to keep you warm in every way. The idea for the monster scarf came in a happy accident. Textile designer Amelie Labarthe, new to a knitting machine, was producing wool samples to make the parts for a teddy. Instead of making the pieces one by one, she knitted all of the parts in a row, intending to cut them later. As an experiment, she made knots with the resulting length of samples, added some eyes, and voilà – Forget Me Knot was born.

Can you turn this knot into a monster?

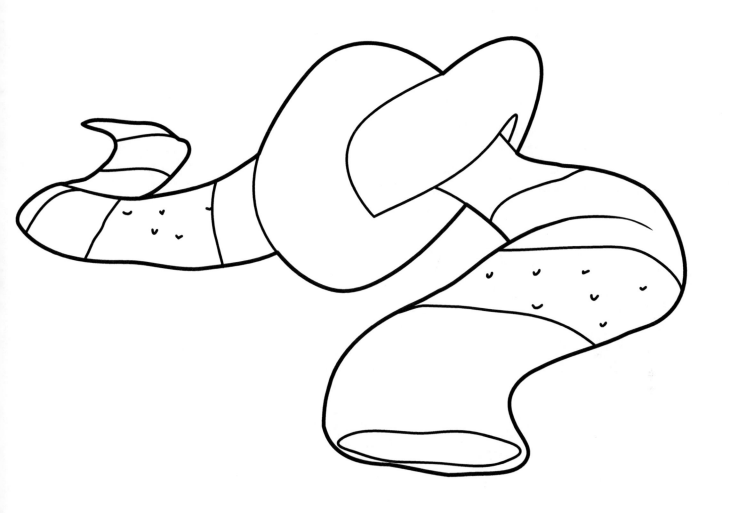

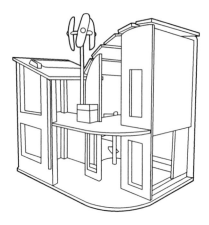

Dimensions (cm): H51 W46 D55
Target Age: 3+
Play Type: Copying, Discovery
[re]strategies: [re]duce, [re]source, [re]spond
Materials: Rubber wood

42 **GREEN DOLLHOUSE**
PLANTOYS

The Green Dollhouse is a completely eco-friendly home featuring alternative fuel sources. It shows little ones how to live in harmony with nature.

All that we are is a result of what we have thought.

Kids can learn how they can protect their environment super-early by playing with the Green Dollhouse. The dollhouse's energy-efficient features include a wind turbine, a solar cell panel and electric inverter for generating electricity, recycling bins, a rain barrel for collecting rain, a biofacade – which uses the natural cycle of plant growth to provide shading – and a blind that can adjust the amount of sunlight and air circulation. Children can learn how to use energy, water and other resources efficiently with the accompanying eco-family characters. The Green Dollhouse, designed by Thitaree Luengtangvarodom and made from rubber wood by PlanToys, has been created in close collaboration with child development specialists. PlanToys are committed to using safe, clean and eco-friendly materials. All their products use rubber wood, which is taken from latex trees felled at the end of their productive life.

Can you furnish the Green Dollhouse?

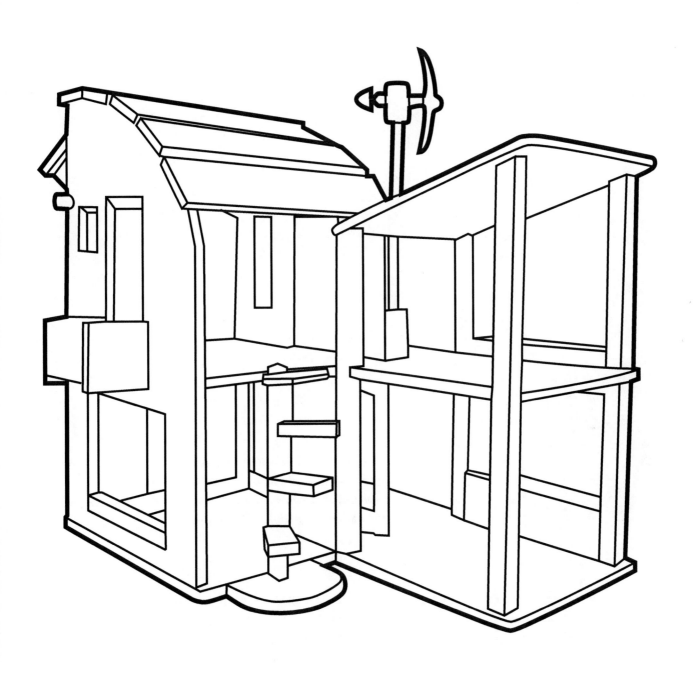

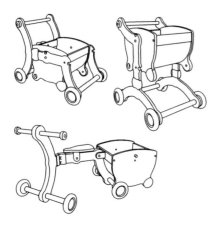

Dimensions (cm): H58 W47 D42 (as baby walker)
Target Age: 9-72 months
Play Type: Copying, Head Spin
[re]strategies: [re]duce, [re]spond
Materials: Plywood, solid wood, natural wood finish,
metal, plastic

44   **GROW UP**
MISHI DESIGN

As a parent and designer I wanted to introduce multi-function products and toys designed in a way so they can be adapted to the various stages of a child's growth.

It's true what they say about kids growing quickly… During the first years of their lives there are many physical and mental changes. With this in mind, Mishael Tzoreff has designed Grow Up – a transformable three in one wooden toy that grows with the child.

Grow Up is first used as a baby-walker when kids take their initial steps, then morphs into a walker-bike and later into a trolley. Easily assembled by an adult, Grow Up is a long lasting toy suitable for kids up to the age of six. Made from plywood and solid wood using CNC (computer numerical-controlled) machines and manually finished by skilled craftsmen, the toy was inspired by Mishael's love of construction and multi-functionality.

Grow Up's aesthetics and ability to adapt to the various stages of a toddler's growth will ensure many years of fun.

Can you match the child to each of the Grow Ups?

Dimensions (cm): H34 W17 D15 (Ursa)
Target Age: 6+
Play Type: Copying
[re]strategies: [re]source, [re]spond
Materials: Beech wood, elastic

46 **HANNO & URSA**
DAVID WEEKS STUDIO

A toy should not only be durable enough to survive the wear and tear of one generation of children – but it should be the kind of toy a father finds in the toy box at his parents' house when looking for something to entertain his own kids.

Designer David Weeks has created a new wooden toy, by connecting Kay Bojesen's iconic teak monkey with the contemporary market of graffiti action figures. David was originally inspired by the television show 'Gilligan's Island' where the Professor was always making practical items out of natural materials like radios out of coconuts. David set out to create a wooden robot, but as he sculpted, the robot turned into a gorilla with a distinct personality, and Hanno was born.

Hanno the Wooden gorilla and Ursa the Wooden bear have powerful hardwood frames with elastic joints that pop and lock into a myriad of poses. The wood used is durable, sustainably harvested, new-growth beechwood. The assembly and mechanic of these toys are obvious and transparent, allowing a child to see and understand their construction. Beautiful and functional, David's toys are built to enjoy generations of play.

Where are Hanno, Hanno Jr and Ursa?
Can you complete the scene?

Dimensions (cm): H59 W44 D1
Target Age: 5+
Play Type: Copying, Discovery
[re]strategies: [re]duce, [re]source, [re]spond
Materials: Wood, cotton

48 **HUNTER GATHERER**
TILEN ZEGULA

Own a pocket knife, climb a tree, throw a spear, play with fire and cook a meal.

Only design if you are absolutely sure it will benefit generations to come.

Hunter Gatherer Educational Toys inspire kids to think outside the fast-food chicken box… and discover more about where animals come from, how plants grow, and how to prepare and cook. Each die-cut wooden educational board is a play-set that needs to be assembled then decorated. They each describe different techniques on how to make tools, live sustainably, and survive independently in the wild!

Children aged five upwards learn to value, appreciate and understand the meaning of nature. Designer Tilen Zegula hopes his product will lead to young people living longer and healthier lifestyles complete with a brand new mindset. Next up for Tilen is the 'modern forager' board, which encourages kids to avoid spending at the supermarket – foraging for food and eating plants from the garden or allotment instead.

Can you match the hunters' tools to their prey?

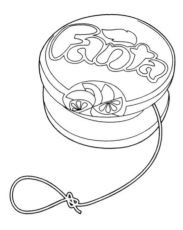

Dimensions (cm): H7 W7 D4
Target Age: 11+
Play Type: Discovery, Head Spin
[re]strategies: [re]spond, [re]use
Materials: Reclaimed drinks can, string, elastic band

50 **ICANIC: YOYO**
JAM

A truly sustainable toy is something that will be around for years to come and still played with or treasured as it's passed down the generations.

A reclaimed drinks can, some string, an elastic band and a few odds and ends for a couple of pence are all the materials you need to make the iCanic yoyo.

Designers at JAM were inspired to make the yoyo after seeing African children create their own toys from disregarded objects and litter. Available as instructions geared at kids aged 11 upwards, the iCanic yoyo gives kids a sense of pride in something they have created

themselves. It teaches sustainable issues and is a social toy, an ice-breaker that requires skill development.

JAM sees kids making iCanics yoyo's and other iCanic art from their favourite graphics, maybe even creating a collection from around the world full of future memories – this yoyo is intended to be treasured. iCanic art will get you reinventing – start small, but think BIG!

Can you match each yoyo to its owner?

Dimensions (cm): Variable
Target Age: 2+
Play Type: Head Spin, Head to Head
[re]strategies: [re]spond
Materials: Mixed-media

52 INTERACTIVE CLIMBING WALL
RAW STUDIO

Don't do it if you don't believe in it.

Kids love climbing. Kids *love* computer games. Designer Nick Rawcliffe has cleverly combined two favourite pastimes to create a 'real life' computer game. Nick's Interactive Climbing Wall features video gameplay projected onto a wall. The player wears special gloves that are detected by an infrared camera and interpreted by positioning software. There is no avatar - the player becomes the character in the scene.
In the Splat the Spider game, the aim is to catch and swat away virtual spiders, avoid obstacles, and beat the clock. The game can challenge any ability of climber even if played on the same wall. The underlying concept is being further developed for other gaming and sports applications. Nick intends to give kids more interesting and athletic things to do in response to the current childhood obesity issue – really good exercise under the guise of a computer game.

Who is on the wall with the climber?
Complete the dot to dot.

Dimensions (cm): H12 W12 D12
Target Age: 7+
Play Type: Copying, Discovery
[re]strategies: [re]create, [re]spond
Materials: Felt, smart fabric, LED, electronics

54 **LOOPIN**
LOST VALUES

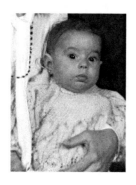

Loopin makes kids appreciate building things; gives them confidence as well as an understanding of how things work.

Be creative, be DIY!

Kids love toys; but they'll love and cherish a toy they've made themselves even more. The Loopin toy kit bridges gender gaps, is fun and educational. Mixing textiles with electronics, it enables kids to make their own soft toy and learn basic electronics in the process. The kit comprises felt, smart fabric, LEDs and electronics. It can be configured to make the Happy or the Grumpy Loopin, and can be remade again and again whilst learning the circuitry. It's one of the few toys on the market that aims to make learning technology appeal to girls too. Currently battery-powered, the designer Elena Corchero is working on future versions that incorporate kinetic and solar power. Once made, the toys are a great talking piece and encourage group activity as the Loopin eyes light up when their smart soft ears are touched together, or to the ears of another Loopin… What's the collective noun for a group of Loopins? A flock, a gaggle or a skool of Loopins?… Anyone?!

Where do Loopins live? Can you draw their home?

Dimensions (cm): Variable
Target Age: 3+
Play Type: Copying, Self-Expression
[re]strategies: [re]create, [re]duce, [re]make, [re]use
Materials: Nylon 66

56 **MAKEDO**
PAUL JUSTIN

It ticks the box on so many areas that are important to me – sustainability, creativity, community and play.

Your world is what you make it.

Wouldn't it be good to make play objects, fantasy figures, costumes, furniture, environments and, well, anything you could think of, all from the materials you found lying around? makedo enables this without the use of a ton of glue or tape so materials can be easily disassembled and reused or recycled. makedo is designed to enable construction with discovered materials, it encourages people to see the creative possibilities in their surroundings while giving them a tool to build.

Re-usability is fundamental to its function – makedo creations can be pulled apart and the materials used over and over again. The makedo product itself is a system of injection-moulded nylon components for cutting and joining found materials into objects and spaces. There are three individual elements – the connector (flexible pin and clip), the hinge (pivoting and lockable) and multi-function tool (for punching and cutting). Just add junk and a little imagination…

What can you make out of junk using makedo?

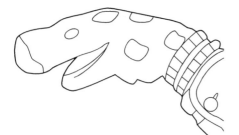

Dimensions (cm): H30 W6 D15
Target Age: 5+
Play Type: Copying, Discovery, Self-Expression
[re]strategies: [re]create, [re]spond, [re]use
Materials: Odd socks, variable

58 **MAKING MATTERS: 101 ODD SOCKS**
EMMA BERRY

If everyone shared their ideas with everyone else, imagine what we would achieve.

What good is an odd sock? Making Matters: 101 Odd Socks looks at ways to save lonely socks from the rubbish bin and educate people in sustainability issues. The Making Matters web-based collective aims to combine sustainable design and education, share ideas, learn through doing and create collective solutions. It takes inspiration from the things we throw away to inform design challenges, inspire solutions and create making projects for kids. Users contribute thoughts, comments and solutions to the Making Matters ideas factories. The 101 Odd Socks challenge gives kids an appreciation of hand-made objects and practical craft skills whilst making use of something considered useless. Playful ways of transforming odd socks proposed so far include MP3 protectors, sock puppets, draft excluders and juggling balls. Get involved – 101 ideas needed!

Can you turn the odd sock into something?

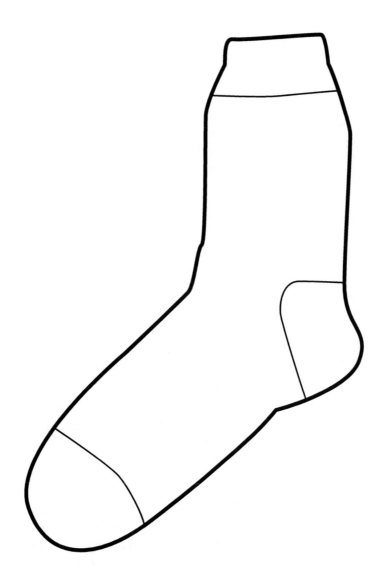

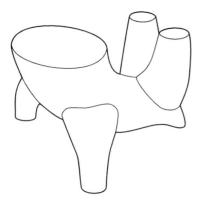

Dimensions (cm): H40 W67 D67
Target Age: Any age
Play Type: Copying, Self-Expression
[re]strategies: [re]duce, [re]make, [re]spond
Materials: Polyethylene

60 **MICO**
EL ULTIMO GRITO

We have been working for a long time around the idea of memory and objects, their representation and their materiality. Investigating how we could use our memories to create links with new ideas, so that a dialogue can be generated.

Mico could be interpreted as an abstract furniture piece, but when played with it takes on a whole new character. The product challenges the rationale behind mainstream design for children. Mico has no specific function as such, it is left up to the child to decide what a Mico is at any given moment. This ability to change encourages multiple interpretations from the child, who can create associations and stories by using the object in play. In this way Mico helps children to explore and develop their own understanding of the world. Mico was created by El Ultimo Grito as part of an exploration of the early stages of child memory development, and is now part of the Me Too collection produced by Italian design company Magis. Made of durable polyethylene, Mico is happy to be ridden on, thrown around, stacked up, dressed up, lent on, sat on, whatever its young owner decides – inside or out.

What could a Mico be?

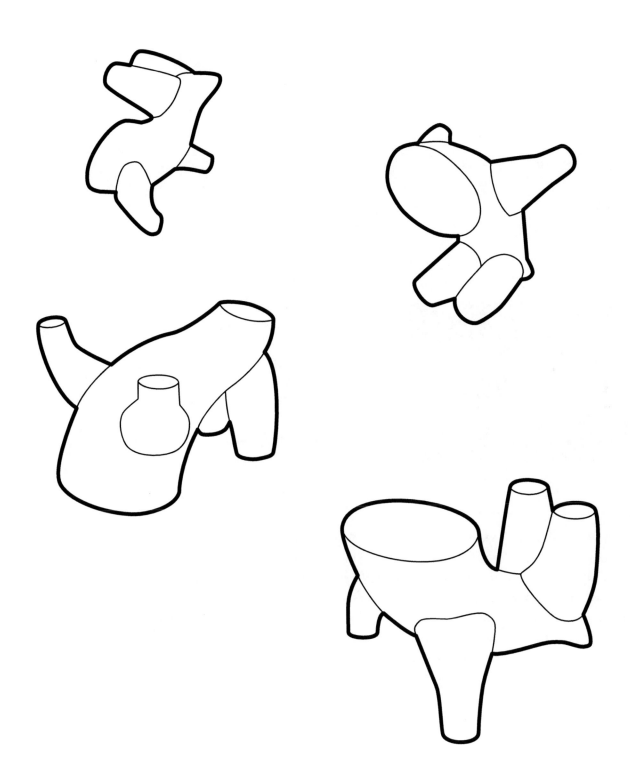

Dimensions (cm): H40 W40 D1
Target Age: From birth
Play Type: Copying, Discovery, Self-Expression
[re]strategies: [re]create, [re]mind, [re]source, [re]use
Materials: Organic T-Shirt, water-based inks

62 **MIMO TEE**
WEMAKE

As a kid Jason had a favourite racing car T-shirt he loved. He tried stretching it to fit, but eventually accepted he had outgrown it and let it go. Mimo Tee is a new way of keeping a favourite item of clothing and turning it into a keepsake toy.

WEmake... you smile, you think, you play, you make!

Kids will love wearing the Mimo monster patterned T-shirt, screen-printed on the back with the WEmake mayhem manifesto for play. And after they've outgrown it, they can turn it into a cuddly toy – instructions included on the inside! Mimo Tee (Mimo's short for My Monster in case you wondered) has a character print on the outside. Mimo's twin can be found on the inside along with instructions on how to transform the top into a cuddly toy.

Simply pair the two sides up, cut and stitch, then use the rest of the organic cotton T-shirt as stuffing. No waste whatsoever and you have your own hand-made monster to give you happy memories for many years to come…

Can you draw the monster's body?

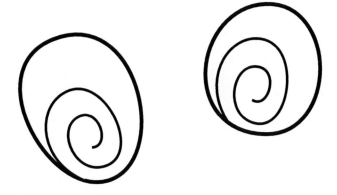

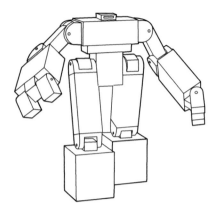

Dimensions (cm): H70 W27 D20
Target Age: 18-36
Play Type: Copying
[re]strategies: [re]claim, [re]mind, [re]spond, [re]use
Materials: Reclaimed timber, steel bolts

64 **MOD:TWO & MOD:ZERO**
SUPERMODIFIEDSTUDIOS

Design is key for creating sustainable solutions, but it must be fully integrated with good business innovation.

Reclaim your space.

MOD:two and MOD:zero designer Nick Mannion has created some super stylised robots that strike a blow for sustainability in the limited edition art toy market – an area that is dominated by vinyl cast products. The MOD series is manufactured from reclaimed sheet material – old tabletops and plywood off-cuts – screen-printed with striking limited edition designs then hand-cut and machined into the component parts of the robot. Due to the high tolerance required, the custom-made joints of

MOD:two are constructed separately using a local CNC machine shop. Parts are then hand-assembled and packaged into reused shoe boxes for delivery.

The MOD series is built on a strong foundation of sustainability, blending the nostalgic appeal of robots and wooden toys, with cutting edge graphics and art toy appeal, in what can only be described as a 'supermodified' way.

What graphics will you add to the Mod:two robot?

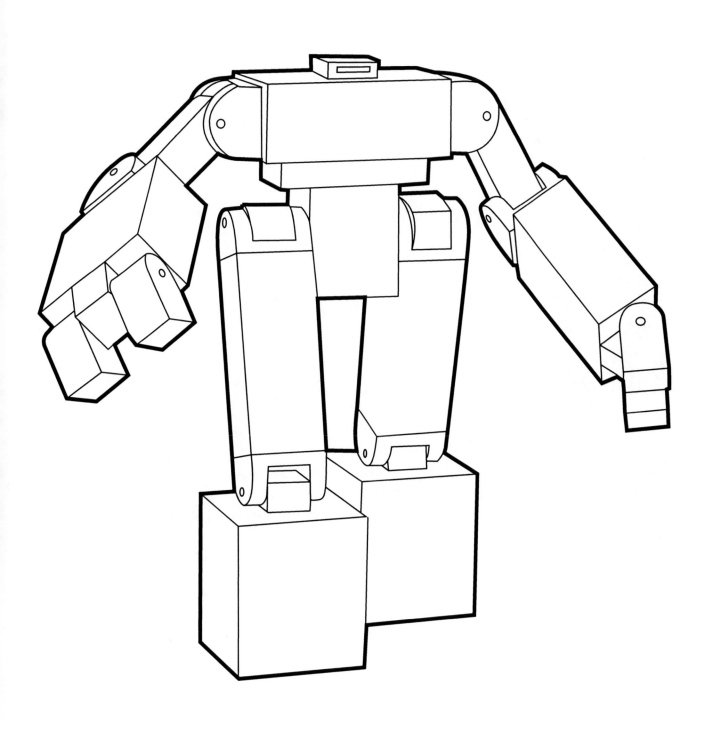

Dimensions (cm): H48 W58 D1
Target Age: 4-14
Play Type: Self-Expression
[re]strategies: [re]create
Materials: Organic cotton

66 MY FIRST WORK OF ART T-SHIRT KIT
EMMA NEUBERG

A colouring-in book you can wear.

Why not wear your own works of art? My First Work of Art print archetypal designs, in outline, on organic cotton garments for kids to paint and add to.

Textile designer Emma Neuberg found children loved to have creative parameters with which to identify; and that with these in place kids flourish and expand into a world of contained imagination and expression. With different sleeve options, neck-lines that can be altered, ruffles, badges and craft kit add-ons, available to purchase at a later stage, the products can be altered and customised. This continued user participation increases product longevity and emotional durability.

The organic fairtrade cotton T-shirts are printed locally with minimal water-based ink. Other products such as cushions and fabric books are planned for the future.

Can you design a T-shirt?

Dimensions (cm): H13 W13 D13
Target Age: Birth+
Play Type: Copying, Discovery
[re]strategies: [re]cycle, [re]source, [re]spond
Materials: Organic Cotton, recycled polyester stuffing,
recycled cardboard packaging

68 MY WONDERCUBE
HELEN TWIGGE-MOLECEY

Watching the pleasure babies get from pulling wet soft wipes from a packet gave me all the inspiration I needed.

A toy is for life — not just for Christmas.

Inspired by the pleasure babies get in pulling wet wipes out of their packet, this soft organic cotton cube has a string of squares with different textures and sounds. Each can be pulled apart, stuck back together and rearranged in any order. Invented by mum-of-three, Helen Twigge-Molecey, it is suitable from birth yet designed to grow with your child. With an extensive choice of add-on fillings – including numbers, letters, animals and storybooks – the adaptability

and versatility of this simple cube makes it a toy that will endure and amuse for years.

My Wondercube is ethically produced, with organic and recycled content and has undergone a full product climate footprint analysis by sustainability experts Giraffe Innovation.

What is coming out of the Wondercube?

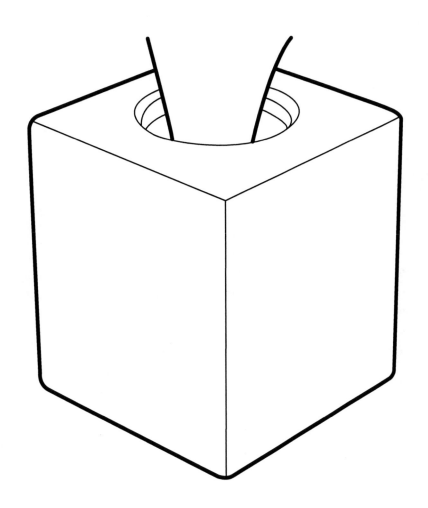

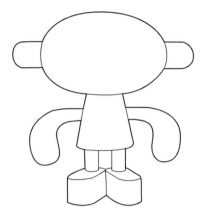

Dimensions (cm): H15 W13 D10
Target Age: 14+
Play Type: Self-Expression
[re]strategies: [re]create, [re]mind, [re]source
Materials: Wood

70 **NEIGHBORWOOD**
MIKE BURNETT

Work hard and be nice to people.

Here's an idea that goes against the grain – a customisable art toy figure made out of wood. Mike Burnett has created this blank wooden sculpture, which allows imaginations to run riot – helping to develop creativity and fine motor skills in style.

Traditionally, art toys are made of rotocast vinyl using a highly toxic manufacturing process. Neighborwood DIY figures are produced in wood with no harmful waste products, and will last long after their vinyl cousins have deformed, faded, and lost their lustre.

Created by Mike Burnett with help from Bigshot Toyworks, a creative studio in the US specialising in the design and production of unique collectables, toys and art objects, Neigborwood DIY figures are designed for big boys and girls aged 14 upwards.

What does your Neighborwood toy look like?

Dimensions (cm): H21 W30 D10 (owl rucksack)
Target Age: 5+
Play Type: Copying, Discovery, Self-Expression
[re]strategies: [re]create, [re]source, [re]spond
Materials: Felt (viscose and wool)

72 OWL RUCKSACK & ROCKET PENCIL CASE
SPARROWKIDS

We believe if children are to learn about the environment, they should work with materials which are friendly to that environment.

A love of nature and the environment, and a dislike of cartoon characters, hero worship and mass merchandising inspired Charlotte Packe to create Sparrowkids DIY educational craft kits. Charlotte wants kids to be impressed and inspired by their natural surroundings. Sparrowkids (the name highlights the demise of the sparrow population) introduces boys and girls to creative crafts with well-designed projects. Making things from the kit range, including a DIY owl rucksack and a cool rocket pencil case, helps develop quiet, meditative play, better hand and eye co-ordination and individuality. Charlottes' sketches of the designs are interpreted on a computer as vector drawings which are sent to die makers. The dies are then used to punch out the component parts from recycled felt and 100% wool. Pieces are assembled into kits, ready to be completed at home.

Can you complete the scene?

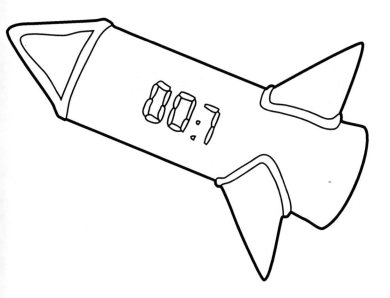

Dimensions (cm): H160 W125 D110 (Teepee)
Target Age: 2-10
Play Type: Copying, Self-Expression
[re]strategies: [re]create, [re]cycle, [re]spond
Materials: Corrugated cardboard

74 PLANE & TEEPEE
PAPERPOD

Inspiration for Paperpod Cardboard Creations came when Christmas and Birthday presents were often discarded so the children could have hours of fun playing with the box!

Some presents have a shorter play life than the cardboard packaging they arrived in – but Paperpod have turned this around. Designer Paul Martin has constructed an imaginative range of toys and furniture out of recycled cardboard for kids aged two to 10. The friendly, affordable designs currently include chairs, a fort, a rocket, a teepee, a doll's house, a playhouse, an aeroplane, a car and signature paperpod. Each offers a blank canvas for children to decorate using paint, collage, pens and crayons. Die-cut from recycled, corrugated cardboard the resulting products are all multi-functional, with lots of play opportunities. They work as a construction toy, a craft toy and a useful piece of furniture or plaything. All products can be folded flat for easy storage. Paperpods can be used in the home, childcare setting or school to create a personal touch, and are ideal for children's parties.

Can you complete the scene?

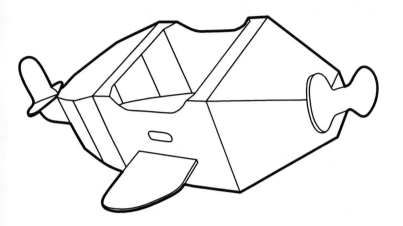

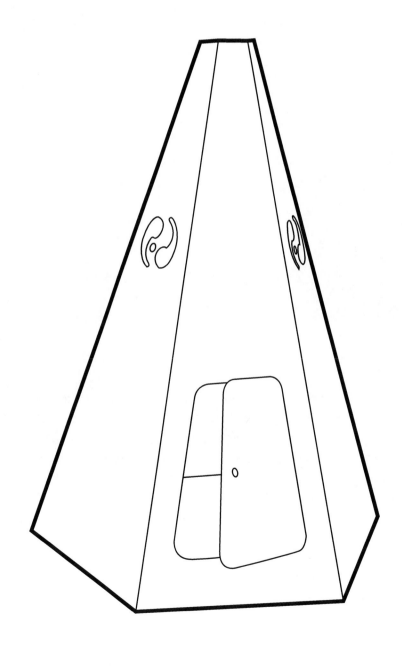

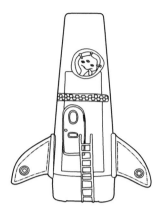

Dimensions (cm): H30 W21
Target Age: 5-12
Play Type: Copying, Self-Expression
[re]strategies: [re]create, [re]spond, [re]use
Materials: Stickers

76 **PLANET NEWPACK**
DAVID STOVELL

Imagination is by far the most important ingredient in a toy.

Manufacturers have to make a profit. If we as designers can help toy manufacturers create a healthy profit through imaginative products, better materials and production methods and better packaging etc along with ethical values, how can they refuse?

Stickers are great. So simple. So coveted by kids. Often used as a reward tool for good behaviour in schools and at home, Planet NewPack stickers aim to encourage play and creative reuse. Designed for five to 12 year-olds, the sticker images of doors, windows, wheels, jets etc. can be applied to domestic waste packaging to create fantasy play objects like houses, castles, and cars. The product encourages the development of the imagination as the child creates new uses for

everyday junk. Designer David Stovell hit on the idea of a tool to help turn waste packaging into fun toys after adapting countless washing-up bottles into monsters, rockets etc. with his own kids.

Planet NewPack has a strong sustainability message for kids as the stickers are cut out and applied to reused containers, encouraging play with found objects and reducing the need for new materials.

What will you turn the milk bottle into?

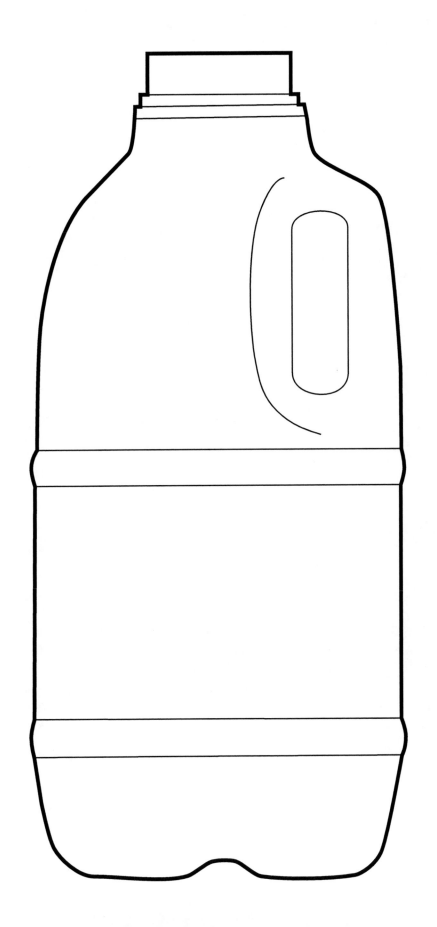

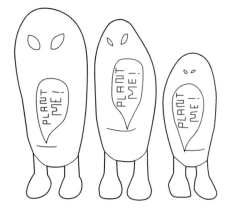

Dimensions (cm): Variable
Target Age: 3+
Play Type: Copying, Discovery
[re]strategies: [re]source, [re]spond
Materials: Latex, growing medium, seeds

78 **PLANT-ME PETS**
MARTÍ GUIXÉ

The Plant-me Pet, with vegetable plant seeds for eyes, is useless until you make it disappear, burying it so that it might grow into an edible food plant. It is a pet that forces you to decide between emotion and function.

We do not need objects, we need functions.

Here's a toy that's sure to grow on you… but only if you decide to plunge its seeded head into some fertile soil.

Because the Plant-me Pets can go one of two ways – they can be colourful collectable toys that are a delight to look at, or they can grow into incredible edibles. Available as a pumpkin, tomato or melon, the Plant-me Pet promotes an understanding of the link between seeds and food.

Hand-made in Spain from bio-degradable latex and packaged in reusable cardboard tubes, the Plant-me Pet explores the abstract differences between emotion and function. Keep it as a pet and let it tap into your emotional side; or make it disappear underground and turn it into something functional – and delicious.

Will you love your pet or eat fresh veg?

What is growing in the plant pot?

Dimensions (cm): H10 W8 D8
Target Age: 7+
Play Type: Copying, Discovery, Self-Expression
[re]strategies: [re]create, [re]cycle, [re]spond
Materials: Pen, pencil, recycled paper, water-based
adhesive

80 **PULP FICTIONS**
STUDIO STEAKHAUS

Sustainable solutions should always be part of the design process, though it needs to be made a priority by industry to truly address our quality of life.

Pulp Fictions is a conceptual design project based on the future availability of home manufacturing using rapid prototyping technology. With Pulp Fictions kids get to create their own action figures. In its current phase children's 2D drawings are digitally modeled into 3D forms by the expert hands of model makers Morpheus. The files are then sent to the Mcor Matrix PRP (Paper Rapid Prototyping) machine. This uses recycled A4 paper to build up the figure, which is cut

and adhered layer by layer. A water-based adhesive is used so the end product can be recycled at end of life.

Erin Deighton from Studio SteakHaus believes there are many directions the project could take in the future, but for now Pulp Fictions poses the intriguing question: what happens when the kids get the keys to the toy factory?

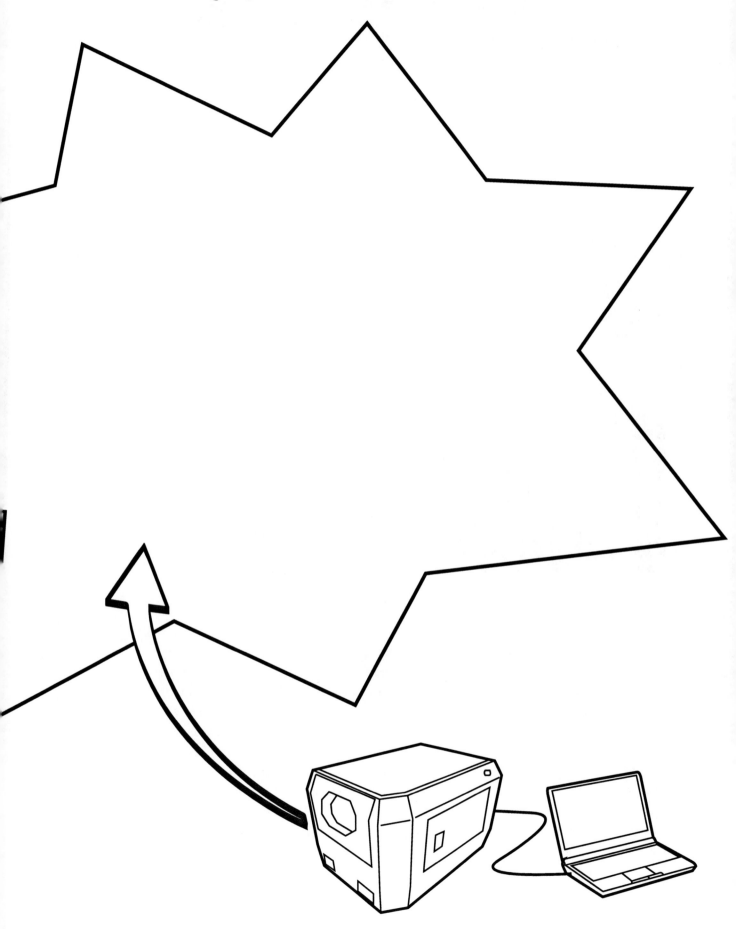

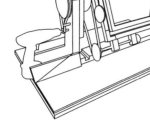

Dimensions (cm): H50 W100 D50
Target Age: 6+
Play Type: Discovery, Self-Expression
[re]strategies: [re]create, [re]source, [re]use
Materials: Scrap, bio-resin

82 **ROTATIONAL MOULDING DIY**
MYFIRST

We had the idea whilst studying to learn more about manufacturing process.

Don't wait around... just give it a go.

Designers Andrew Duffy and Craig Tyler wanted to understand more about the industrial process of rotational moulding, so went and built a miniature machine from scrap materials to replicate the process. They haven't looked back and have been using their machine to rotocast hollow toys from re-used packaging waste and bio-resin – the Something Old Something New range. Once a packaging piece suitable to use as mould has been found, it is inserted into the machine.

Canonbury Arts bio-resin is injected into the mould, which is spun using a cordless drill until the material sets. An important message behind MyFirst design is that anyone has the ability to reuse what is already around them. The Rotational Moulding DIY machine is available as a set of instructions so big kids can make their own. Craig and Andrew are also looking at producing a flat-pack version. Either way, their inspiring design enables kids to have their own little toy factory.

What would you make in the Rotational Moulding DIY machine?

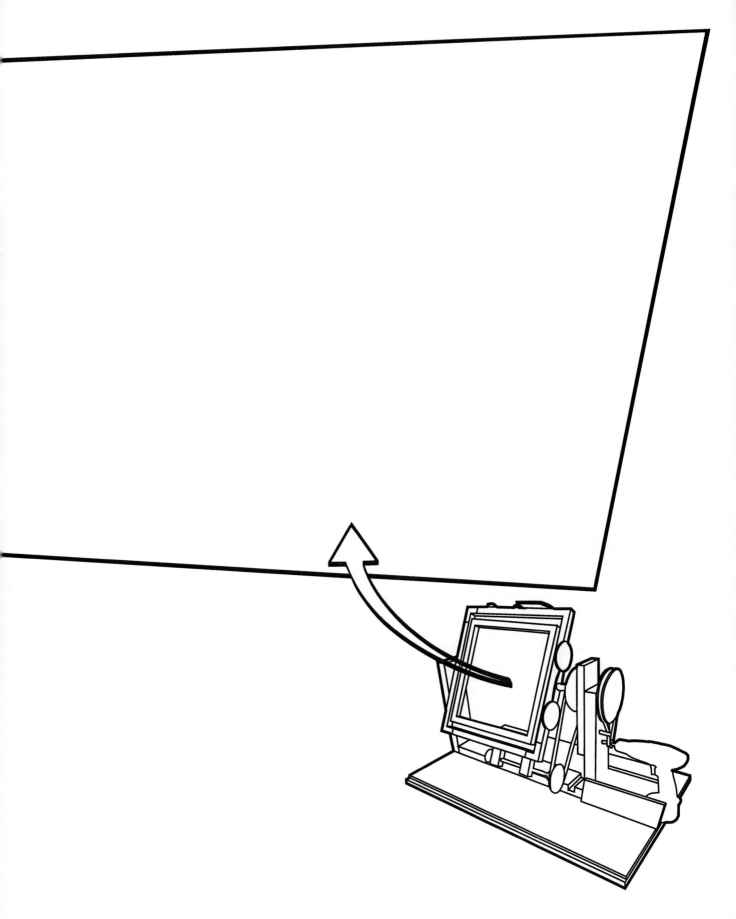

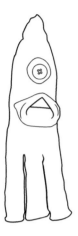

Dimensions (cm): H33 W5 D5
Target Age: 6-60
Play Type: Copying, Self-Expression
[re]strategies: [re]create, [re]spond, [re]use
Materials: Recycled paper, recycled cardboard tube,
reused buttons, needle, thread

84 **SOCK ALIEN KIT**
REMAKE ME

I get frustrated by the amount of packaging around kids' toys and the throwaway nature of the toys themselves.

Remake Me designer Lizzie Lee is on a crusade to reincarnate the UK's hundreds and thousands of odd, holey or worn socks so they can go on to live happy new lives as much-loved sock aliens! Lizzie's Sock Alien Kits consist of sewing supplies with tapestry needle, thread and some buttons to use for eyes. Also included is an A3 poster with step-by-step instructions on one side and a picture of some alien friends to colour in on the other, plus inspiration to turn the kit's cardboard tube packaging into a space rocket. All that needs to be supplied is an odd sock, a cereal packet and some stuffing. Inspired by a desire to teach kids how to recycle, be resourceful and create enthusiasm in both boys and girls for sewing, the kits are suitable for those aged six plus. The kit encourages kids to be imaginative and think twice about throwing away things that can be fixed or reused as something else. Sock Alien makers can show off their creation in an online gallery.

Can you draw a sock alien?

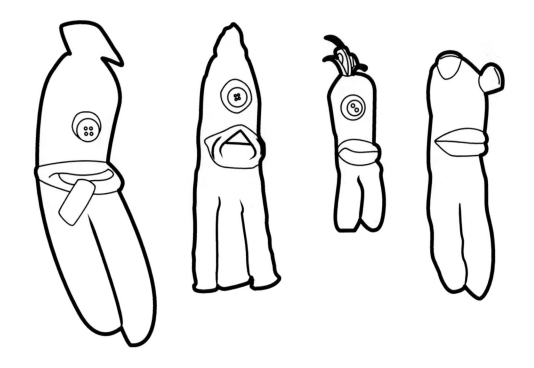

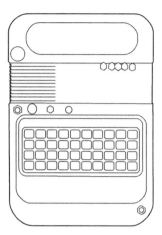

Dimensions (cm): H25 W18 D3
Target Age: 19-65
Play Type: Chance, Self-Expression
[re]strategies: [re]mind, [re]spond, [re]use
Materials: Switches, potentiometers, LEDs, wire, solder,
blood, sweat, tears

86 **SPEAK & SPELL**
CIRCUITBENZ

It's all about finding new ways to use
discontinued technology.

By changing the use of Speak & Spell,
a new market can be created that will
support a fertile cottage industry of
like-minded engineers.

Back in the 80s it taught us to speak and
spell, but thanks to some serious noughties'
tweakage, it can do so much more.

The Circuitbenz Speak & Spell is now a bizarre
and brilliant musical instrument after designer
Ed Chocolate rewired the classic educational
toy and turned it into a sampler's electronic
heaven. The familiar shape of the original toy
design, the limitations of the voice chip and its
electronic and physical robustness, incredibly,

lend itself to unusual sonic possibilities. It
produces all sorts of weird and wonderful
noises with bizarre loops, robotic chanting,
and strange alien noises spewing out of the
speakers.

The Circuitbenz Speak & Spell is already
gaining popularity with many electronic
musicians but will be enjoyed by anyone who
likes to play with strange, crazy sounds.

What sound is the Speak & Spell making?

Dimensions (cm): Variable
Target Age: 3+
Play Type: Copying, Self-Expression
[re]strategies: [re]claim, [re]mind, [re]spond
Materials: Reclaimed and vintage fabric

88 **STUFFYOURDOODLES**
LUCY MOOSE

I love working with textiles and solving puzzles through using them in a 3D way. It's so much fun, and I love the fact they make people laugh.

StuffYourDoodles does exactly that... it turns your drawings into fun, laugh-out-loud 3D textile toys. Kids send in their character blueprint to designer Lucy Moose, and a stuffed version of their doodle is faithfully created. No doodle is too impossible and orders to date include a green one-eyed beast holding a bundle of triangles, a multicoloured dog with large red lips and black ears, and an alien guy with big teeth. The end results are always charming and distinctive.

Each one-off design, created in the mind of a child, is personal to its owner, and encourages drawing and design skills as kids see their design become 'real'. StuffYourDoodles toys come with their own label showing the original doodle sketch.

These fun toys, made from recycled and vintage fabric, are great for creative play, wonderful to touch, and make everyone who sees them smile.

Can you design a soft toy?

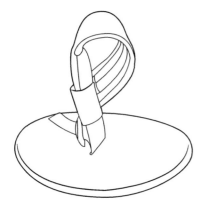

Dimensions (cm): H30 W20 D35
Target Age: 2-6
Play Type: Head Spin
[re]strategies: [re]spond
Materials: Birch ply, nylon webbing, neoprene

90 **SWING ARM**
ALON MERON

Make the most of the body you live in.

I began to think about sustainability by moving to a new country with the content of two suitcases and realising I didn't need much more than that.

Why not be the most exhilarating toy in the box? Swing Arm is a fantastically simple, fun toy that turns the arm of the parent into a toy swing, allowing exciting play for toddlers. Designer Alon Meron was inspired by his father-in-law, 'a great big man and a human swing for his grandchildren' to create a product that enabled other people to play with confidence, whilst countering the over-protection of children and absurd health and safety regulations. Swing Arm consists of a round disc-shaped seat for kids to sit on and a centre handle for the adult swing operator to grip. Built to last and endure many years of active play, the seat is made of laminated birch ply and the handle is made by sewing nylon webbing with foam and neoprene padding. Encouraging adult-toddler activity where the parent becomes a source of extreme fun for the child, Swing Arm play is fast, energetic and will keep you fit! Go on, get out there and swing!

Can you draw yourself on the Swing Arm?

Dimensions (cm): H14 W7 D7
Target Age: From birth
Play Type: Discovery, Self-Expression
[re]strategies: [re]cycle, [re]mind
Materials: Placenta, stuffing

92 **TWIN TEDDY KIT**
ALEX GREEN

The Twin Teddy Kit is a unique and personal toy which celebrates the unity of the infant, the mother, and the placenta.

A placenta teddy? Designer Alex Green argues why not? The placenta and baby have, after all, shared a unique bond together. What if they were never parted? The Twin Teddy Kit transforms the placenta from medical waste by-product to a loveable soft bear using a home tanning process. It makes use of a very natural material and is recycling at its very best! Once revered as the companions and protectors of babies, in medieval times placentas were buried as a symbolic gesture to tie infants to their homeland. But Western culture has lost these rituals and today placentas are routinely discarded.

To make the suede-like material for the bear's skin, the placenta is cut in half and rubbed with sea salt to cure it. It is then dried out, before being treated with an emulsifying mixture of tannin and egg yolk to make it soft and pliable before being laid to dry in the sun.

Can you match each teddy to its twin?

A ___

B ___

C ___

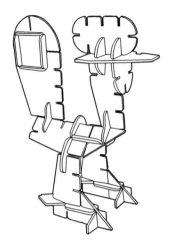

Dimensions (cm): Variable
Target Age: 7+
Play Type: Copying, Self-Expression
[re]strategies: [re]cycle, [re]spond
Materials: 3-ply recycled cardboard

94 **TOTEM**
KIDSONROOF

Create! Don't just consume.

Be unique, feel free, love the world and your close ones, respect nature and be the creator of your own life.

How can you NOT think about sustainability these days?

Rockets, butterflies, dragonflies, chickens, spiders, trees, boats… whatever takes your fancy, you can probably create in the recycled cardboard Totem world. Kidsonroof designer couple Romy Boesveld and Ilya Yashkin came up with the 3D Totem world idea thanks to some humble cardboard boxes, scissors and precious playtime with their son. The Totem building pieces are made from sturdy cardboard and paper printed with Kidsonroof's own unique style of graphics.

There are swords, dragons, flowers, coins, animals, plants, and secret symbols hidden in their designs. Sets available include Totem City, Totem Nature, Mini Totem and Totem Tree of Life. Each theme has suggested models and a myriad of open building opportunities. And as all Totem pieces are compatible, and recyclable, the possibilities really are endless.

What can you create using Totem?

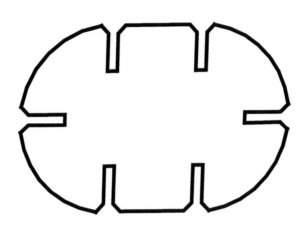

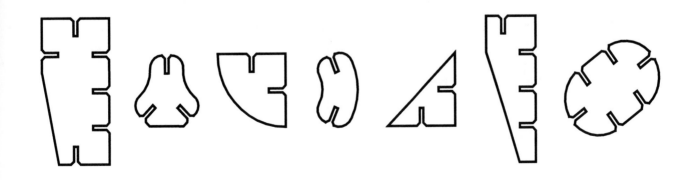

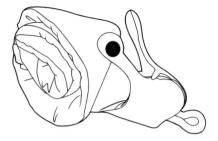

Dimensions (cm): Variable
Target Age: 6 months +
Play Type: Copying
[re]strategies: [re]duce, [re]spond
Materials: Recycled fibre felt, bamboo fabric, cotton,
silicone, EVA foam

96 **UAK: UNITED ANIMAL KINGDOM**
YASUKOBELL DESIGN

Design with passion and with a firm
purpose to make people smile.

Don't panic!

Is it a fun soft toy? Or a baby play mat?
Inspired by designer Yasuko Bell's happy
memories of rolling around on a futon as a
child – the United Animal Kingdom (UAK)
product is both.

Made from recycled fibre felt, bamboo fabric,
cotton, silicone and EVA foam, there are
currently two UAK creatures, the snail and
the rhino, but the United Animal Kingdom
has plans to grow its animal population.

Offering a comfortable environment for play,
it also encourages children to learn character
making.

Yasuko developed the dual function of the
product by closely watching how children
interacted with the toy, making modifications
accordingly. Made with longevity in mind, the
duality of the UAK means once the baby mat
is no longer required, it continues to be used
as a playful soft toy.

Can you draw where the UAK creatures live?

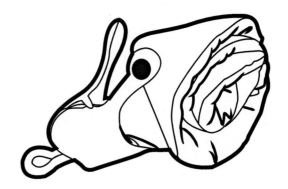

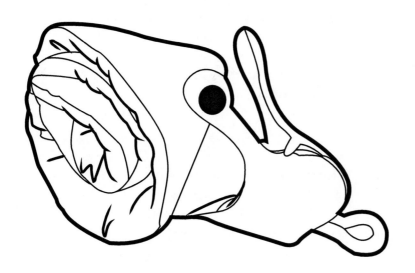

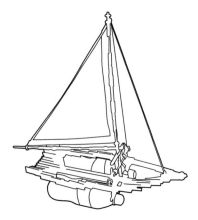

Dimensions (cm): Variable
Target Age: 6-99
Play Type: Copying, Discovery, Self-Expression
[re]strategies: [re]create, [re]make, [re]use
Materials: Plastic

98 **ÜBERSTIX**
ÜBERSTIX

Uberstix does not require the endless purchasing of new licensed products; a few Uberstix and some common household items can keep kids busy for months.

You can look at anything and see the potential for improvement.

Don't bin that cup! Or that straw. The wooden lolly-stick will work great as a mast for your sailboat.

Uberstix toys are engineered to mate with common household recyclables and make "up-cycling" fun for kids! The system's eight different components can be connected to construct, well, just about anything a young mind dreams up. The sailboats really sail, and the planes really do fly!

Designer Dane Scarborough found it unsettling that so many kids may never have the opportunity to develop some of their potential. Building toys help develop spatial skills, problem solving and visualisation. A child with little money can buy just a few Uberstix and use other items to expand their toy chest, rather than being forced to continue buying new products each time one project is finished.

Can you complete the dot to dot to find out what's added to the bottle?

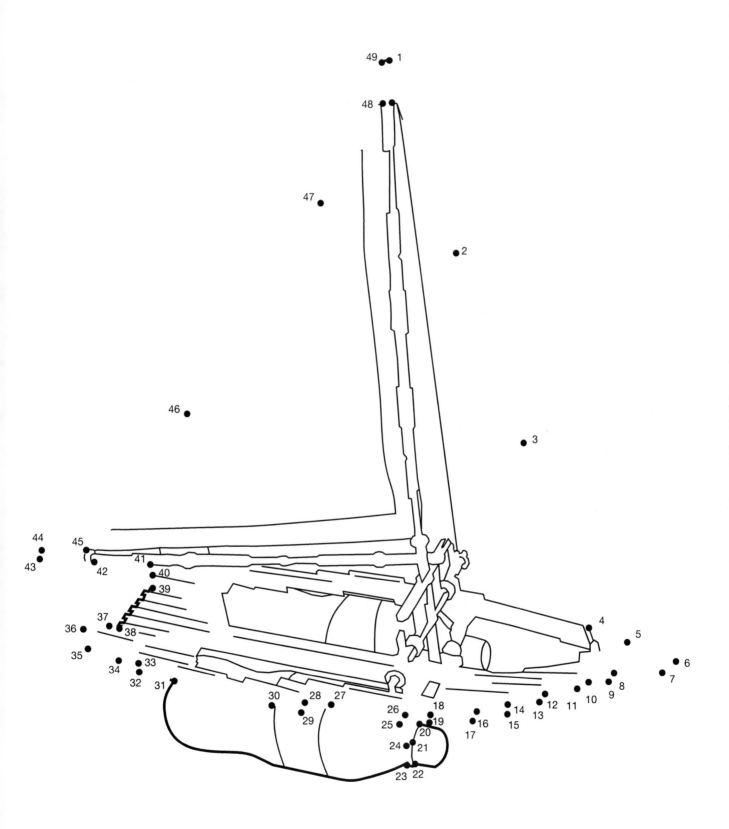

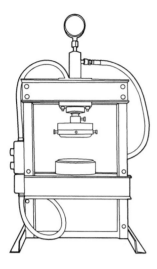

Dimensions (cm): H14 W14 D2 (frisbee)
Target Age: Any
Play Type: Discovery, Head Spin
[re]strategies: [re]cycle, [re]spond
Materials: Milk cartons

100 **UP-CYCLED FRISBEE**
FUTURE INDUSTRIES

Children will be able to see first-hand how their toy has been manufactured purely from milk cartons. This will serve as a powerful educational lesson and hopefully encourage them to recycle more in the future.

Hot off the press, quite literally, are these Up-cycled Frisbees made using a nifty heat pressing machine by design company Future Industries. Used milk cartons are washed and then shredded into chips. The chipped plastic is then placed between two heated aluminium moulds and put under pressure. The moulds are then cooled with water and hey presto, the frisbee is created! The production process is educational and gives children a greater connection with the plastic frisbee, encouraging them to recycle. The Future Industries machine came about when designers Ben Atkinson-Willes and Charlie Crook began looking at how plastic is recycled. They wanted to see if they could develop new ideas to increase people's ability and desire to recycle. They hope to develop a system where people can bring in plastic and have it recycled there and then into a product of their choice.

Can you draw a better circle than Olly in the perfect circle competition?

Rules:

Draw a circle as neat as you can, whoever draws the most perfect circle wins! Don't forget to write your name next to your circle. Get your friends to have a go too.

Dimensions (cm): H46 W55 D102 (trike)
Target Age: 1-5
Play Type: Head Spin
[re]strategies: [re]cycle, [re]duce, [re]source, [re]spond
Materials: Sustainable birch plywood, recycled plastic
wheels, rubber, non-toxic finishes, certified organic
cotton, recycled packaging

102 WISHBONE BIKE
WISHBONE DESIGN STUDIO

I wanted a running bike that my just-walking son could actually use!

My own favourite toy was my bike because of the freedom it gave me, the enjoyment I got from fixing it and the lifestyle it encouraged.

This three in one Wishbone Bike by designer Richard Latham evolves with the different stages of child development from age one up to age five. Starting at age one as a lightweight stable trike without pedals, it converts to a bike teaching two and three year-olds how to balance on two wheels without the need for stabilisers. By the age of four to five, the frame flips over, making it one of the largest balance bikes on the market.

The Endangered Species Limited Edition Wishbone Bike takes its inspiration from New Zealand's rare, carnivorous giant kauri snail, and highlights the need to protect biodiversity for future generations.

Built to last and to be handed down to a younger sibling or relative or kid down the street, every Wishbone Bike has the potential to become an heirloom.

Which Wishbone Bike is riding to each house?

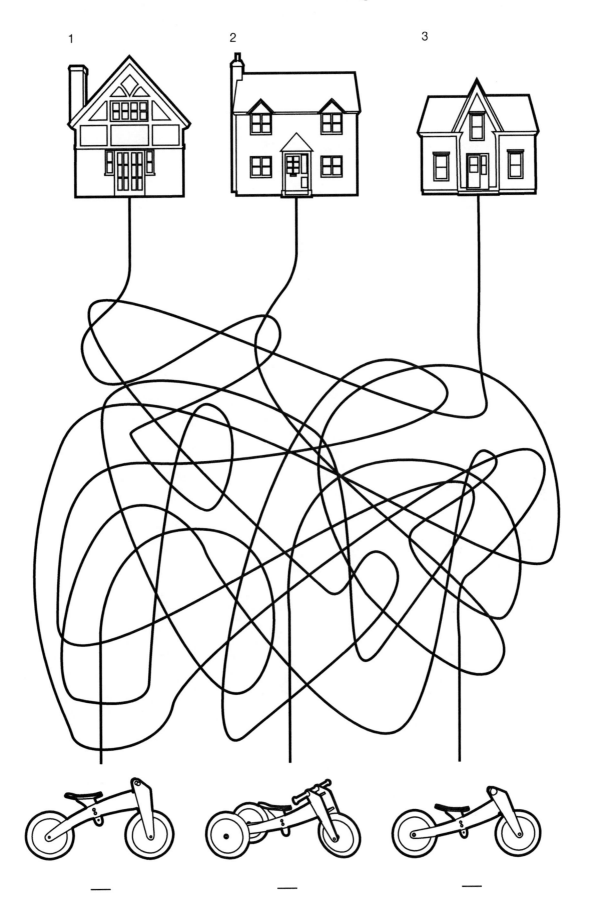

Dimensions (cm): H   W   D
Target Age:
Play Type:
[re]strategies:
Materials:

104   **PRODUCT NAME:**
DESIGNER NAME:

DESCRIPTION:

Design your own sustainable toy!

PLAY TYPES

The play types identified in this book come from Flowmaker: A Design Tool. Flowmaker defines play as "an activity that absorbs us mentally and physically, elevating our emotions". Flowmaker play type definitions:

Chance:	Choosing to surrender to uncontrollable events.
Copying:	Role-play, mimic, tell stories, parody, impersonate.
Discovery:	Learning, uncovering, deducing, investigating.
Head Spin:	Dizziness, light-headedness, rush, vertigo.
Head to Head:	Contest, challenge, struggle, tournament.
Self-Expression:	Creative, imaginative response to the world.

Further recommended reading on play theory:
Flowmaker: A Design Tool by WEmake (2004) ISBN 0-9547337-0-3
Homo Ludens by Johan Huizinga (1950) ISBN 0-8070-4681-7
Man, Play and Games by Roger Caillois (1958) ISBN 0-252-07033-X
The Ambiguity of Play by Brian Sutton-Smith (1997) ISBN 0-674-01733-1

[RE]STRATEGIES

Since 2005 [re]design has been using nine [re]strategies
to help explain and encourage different approaches to
sustainable design.

[re]claim: Designs using waste materials in the raw, without
reprocessing.

[re]create: Customised or personalisable designs – making an emotive
connection between owner and object.

[re]cycle: Designs made with reprocessed waste materials.

[re]duce: Designs which minimise waste of energy and materials,
are multifunctional, or raise awareness of resource use.

[re]make: Designs that allow easy, cost-effective disassembly
and re-use of parts or recycling at end of life.

[re]mind: Characterful designs that evoke memories, reminding you
to treasure them.

[re]source: Designs using renewable natural materials, managed
to ensure a sustainable supply.

[re]spond: Sociable designs which invite interaction and friendliness.

[re]use: Designs making creative use of readymade, second-hand
objects and components.

[re]design is a social enterprise that propagates sustainable actions through design. We partner with a wide range of organisations to pioneer strategic approaches to sustainable design and help bring concepts to fruition.

As climate change demonstrates the urgency of sustainable behaviour change, [re]design sets out to decouple eco-awareness from doom and gloom. The need for environmental action is an opportunity to ask how we can create true quality of life, now and for the future. The questions posed by sustainability challenge designers to develop different answers: new ideas, aesthetics, making processes, applications of technologies and materials, and ways of relating to products.

Within this evolving design landscape, [re]design highlights the work of designers taking a diverse range of approaches towards sustainability. We translate these approaches into principles that can be shared with other designers and businesses, helping sustainable design to grow. [re]design aims to engage, inform, inspire and empower diverse audiences – public, education and business – to make greener choices.

ABOUT US

SARAH JOHNSON FOUNDING DIRECTOR

Sarah is an entrepreneurial, enthusiastic communicator with a passion for strategic design and its potential to enable social and environmental change in the world. She came to design late, seeking a more positive role in the world after an early career in financial services marketing. Sarah facilitates, encourages and completes positive design actions through her work as designer, curator and event organiser.

JASON ALLCORN CREATIVE DIRECTOR

Jason is a skilled designer, maker and semi-reformed skip diver! He has a wealth of experience developing and delivering front-end concept and ideation workshops. Doing it for the Kids has allowed the former Lego concept lab consultant to combine his passions for play and sustainable design. Jason regularly delivers workshops and lectures on creative thinking and sustainable design strategies.

Big thanks to the [re]design team – Olly, Sam, Alex, Jon, Marty and Matt – for a sterling effort in designing, researching, and pulling this project together on a tiny budget. To our good friends Lou and Paul we are indebted for fabulous copywriting, proofreading, pruning and punning.

We would also like to acknowledge an inspiration for the design of this book. We have always loved The Anti-Colouring Book by Susan Striker and Edward Kimmel. This classic from 1978 strove to "…rekindle the excitement of fantasy, to reawaken the senses, and to reaffirm individuality and self-expression." We hope we've achieved a little of that too!

THANK YOU

WWW.REDESIGNDESIGN.ORG

Lightning Source UK Ltd.
Milton Keynes UK
19 September 2009

143928UK00001B/56/P